MW00987953

Leadership
Starts With You

Written By
John Barrett

Published by
Rocket Publishing

Published By: Rocket Publishing

Book Design By: John Barrett

Thanks:
My amazing wife, Erin, our two beautiful daughters, Zion & Allie, and our little guys, Isaiah & Henry. They teach me more about leadership than anyone else ever could. To everyone who helped bring this book together with their appreciated input. To my mentor, Dr. John C. Maxwell, for showing me the way.

CONTENT:

Your Field Guide

Navigating leadership can be a confusing and overwhelming journey. There is uncharted territory to get lost in. Seemingly insurmountable mountains to climb. And life-threatening rapids to endure, just to mention a few. And don't let me forget the unforeseen challenges that arise every morning to greet your workload. No wonder most people placed in a "leadership" position tend to quit within the first year. The journey becomes more than we bargained for, and sometimes, even our physical health suffers if we are not careful.

I have coached leaders for over twenty years and have seen just about every situation you can imagine when it comes to people coming and going into leadership. I have discovered that most leaders, especially young leaders, get thrown into a wilderness of challenges without guidance. There is no compass to help them navigate through the peaks and valleys of their responsibilities. Therefore, they feel lost, afraid, alone, and disillusioned at what they thought would be a career-advancing trek. This is where I come in...enter your leadership coach and guide.

Every leader needs a guide to help bring out the best in them. Luke had Yoda, Katniss had Haymitch, Frodo had Gandolph, Dorothy had Glenda, and the list goes on. Everyone needs a trusted coach to help them unleash the hero they were created to be. I do just that. My role is to catapult your leadership ability and level up your success.

Though I wish we could spend one-on-one time to help you where you are specifically, I have done the next best thing I can do. I have compiled a field guide to serve as a compass for your leadership journey. This field guide identifies some of the most critical lessons every leader needs to know to find the truth north of leadership. This guide will be your personal compass to help guide you toward success in your leadership adventure.

I hope you dive in and allow these principles to impact your leadership, even if you just need to be reminded of what's essential for leading yourself.

Enjoy!

(1)

Live
With
Purpose

Leaders are purpose-driven people.

Knowing what you should be doing helps you realize if you should be doing what it is you are doing. Purpose is *the* filter for knowing if you are spending your time in the right ways. It gives us an internal compass to navigate your schedule. In a comprehensive study on time management, *Wall Street Journal* best-selling author David Finkel found that the average person wastes more than 30% of their workweeks on "low value and no value activities." He went on to say, "Total that up and we're looking at 21.8 wasted hours each week -- hours that are going up in smoke while you're doing things that contribute little to no value to your company. Depending on the length of your workweek, those wasted hours could account for as much as one-third of your time."

If your actions don't align with your purpose, you must be willing to let it go. My mentor, Dr. John C. Maxwell, says, "You have to give up in order to go up." As purpose-driven people, We can't get preoccupied with temptations that pull us away from what we need to do. But unfortunately, too many people are stuck doing what they don't want to do rather than freely living the life they are meant to do.

Every day, you should be getting one step closer to winning. Every play should drive you to your target. Every meeting should be purposeful. Every task should align with your organization's values. When your eyes are fixed on your target, nothing should distract you from it. The word distraction means "to be pulled apart." The word depicts a medieval type of torture method where a person would be pulled apart at the seams of their limbs by being tied to four horses going in opposite directions. This technique became known as "Death by Distraction." We cannot allow ourselves to be distracted from the goals set before us. Everyone faces distractions in life, but identifying and moving past them is the key. Drive your performance in the straightest line possible to your target by eliminating unnecessary distractions. When you determine your purpose, you bring clarity to what your daily duties need to be.

You need to be very strategic and selective about using your time. You need to think of time as an investment of purpose. Only invest in the things that give you the greatest return. Time is precious, so invest it wisely. Benjamin Franklin said, "Dost thou love life? Then do not squander time, for that is the stuff life is made of."

There are three types of people when it comes to time:

VICTIMS OF THEIR TIME

These are the people being beaten up and knocked out by their schedules. They are unable to say "No," so they are consumed with "stuff" cluttering their lives. These people have no defense against the time stealers robbing them of productivity. They over-schedule and over-commit themselves to more than they can handle. Victims must stand up and defend their time, or they will be slaughtered by it. Don't invest your life into things that will never make a difference in the end.

MANAGERS OF THEIR TIME

These people only keep their heads above water, treading back and forth. They are not getting ahead in life; they are just maintaining what they have. Managers usually just keep their lives from getting too crazy. They focus on keeping the ship afloat and do their best to throw any extra water in the boat back out. Most people feel that they are doing well if they manage their time. But they never really feel like they have the capacity to do the things they want to do because the immediate demands suck up every ounce of energy.

LEADERS OF THEIR TIME

These are the people who make time work for them. They control their time; their time doesn't control them. They are focused on getting the things done that really matter and will yield a fruitful harvest from their labor. They do not waste their time on good things; they spend most of their time on the best things that only they can do. They delegate the rest to others or surrender it all together. Leaders of their time do what they feel "called" to do and what they are "purposed" to do. These people don't just wake up to an alarm clock; they wake up to a calling.

Every day counts, so make the most of it and aspire to be a leader of your time. Only do what you should be doing. Get intentional about using your time wisely. Even more importantly, make sure you determine your purpose. I have coached many people over the years through the process of deciding their unique purpose individually and as a leader. And it first starts with leading your time so you can have the margin to invest your time in self-discovery. The greater you know yourself, the greater you can grow yourself into the leader you are. Your compass should direct your destination, and your clock should direct your daily duties to get there.

2

Grow Thyself

If I asked you, "What is your growth plan?" What would the response be? Would you be able to give me a quick and precise answer? If you hesitate or have to think hard about it, I have bad news for you…you probably don't have a growth plan.

The most successful people know exactly what they are doing to develop themselves. They have thought through the process and implemented a system that creates a greenhouse effect of growth. They can tell you what their growth plan is very quickly and precisely because of the effort they have put into it.

You too should have a specific growth plan for yourself.

Growth is not an automatic process. We don't get better without intentional effort. A growth plan is a game changer for your career and impact if you choose to develop yourself like never before. This could be the moment your future self thanks you for the rest of your life. So, what are you going to do to improve your skills as a leader? What will you do to go to a new level in your abilities?

Here are four lessons you must get if you are going to grow to your maximum potential:

LESSON #1: BREAK DOWN YOUR LEARNING INTO GROWTH CATEGORIES

Do you remember the old school choose your own adventure books when you were younger? I loved these books because you got to control the story. It was such an interactive way of engaging the reader to feel like you were really in the story deciding your fate. Growth is much like a choose-your-own-adventure book. You get the power to determine the fate of your future self. You can invest in your success, depending on how much you put into it. What you output in life is a direct result of what you input. So get ready to choose your own adventure.

You can't learn what you need to know until you know what you need to learn. So first, you need to choose categories of specific areas you want to grow in this year. These topics will guide you as you select the books, articles, podcasts, etc… you need to surround yourself with. For example, I have five categories that help me choose all my resources for my growth plan:

- Faith
- Psychology
- Leadership
- Business
- Innovation

Each month I pick five book resources that I will learn and study that correspond with each category. So by the end of the month, I have read five books that are helping me develop in these areas I have determined of most importance to me. Now that is my plan, but you need to choose the specific categories you want to study and develop. Mine are general topics because of how I do my plan, but yours may be more specific such as communication, conflict resolution, problem-solving, etc... Whatever you do, make sure you pick some intentional skills you want to get great at.

LESSON #2: COLLECT YOUR RESOURCES

If you are going to maximize your potential, you need resources that will help you. Once you determine the categories you want to learn about, you must gather what you need. You do this by:

- Researching the best resources in the area you want to learn in
- Asking others (that you respect) what resources they are learning from
- Curiously hunting for something worth learning about

You see, you have to consume your mind with information, for it will lead to transformation.

The mind acts as a cognitive library storing information from everything you encounter. As your conscious mind experiences stimuli, your subconscious stores the data in a very deep and detailed system. Think of your mind as a library with thousands of categories where you have been and are cataloging every-thing you experience. As you experience something, your mind instantly goes to work writing what you're learning into a book stored on the shelf of that category.

For example, what comes to mind if I tell you to think of Africa? Most likely, you are thinking of Elephants, safaris, the natives, deserts, etc... When I told you to think of Africa, your mind went to the shelf labeled Africa, and you pulled out a book of information you have been writing your whole life. You may have thought of particular things about Africa based on your experience, especially if you've been there or lived there. I instantly think of some friends who live in Africa, along with many other images I have associated in my Africa book. The more experiences and information you have concerning Africa, the more you can access it.

We don't go to our potential as though it is waiting for us somewhere; we grow to our potential by learning day by day. Oliver Wendell Holmes said, "One's mind, once stretched by a new idea, never regains its original dimensions." So as you journey through resources, your mind will stretch with examples, tips, and strategies to empower your leadership ability. Your cognitive awareness will become a leadership library archive when you are filled with ideas. You will then be able to access this library in any given situation and know how to lead through it. As your cognitive leadership library increases, it catapults your ability to lead effectively.

This is why leaders are readers; they constantly fill their minds with quotes, stories, experiences, stats, and ideas to level up. Great leadership starts with information, and this information leads to transformation. The transformation begins in them first and then transforms the world around them.

Collect resources and start to consume them every moment you can.

LESSON #3: CREATE YOUR SYSTEM

You are only as good as your system. Most people have lots of things they want to learn, but they don't have a system to help them ensure they actually do it. If you don't systemize your growth plan, you'll likely never follow through with it. You can't just say, "I want to read more." Or "I want to watch more TED talks." or "I want to take some courses to learn." You have to turn it into a real challenge for yourself that has a place and time on the calendar.

The first thing I would ask you if we were sitting down is, "When do you intentionally take time to grow?" If you don't tell me a specific time on the calendar you do this...you probably don't. The most dedicated growers have a space in their schedule for growth. For me, I wake up each morning Monday-Friday and dedicate 30-60 minutes to my growth plan. The first thing I do when I wake up is go to my chair and take out the book I am going to read that morning.

I told you (Lesson #1) that I have five categories I grow in (Faith, Psychology, Leadership, Business, Innovation/Creativity). Each month I collect (Lesson #2) five books that I will read for that month. I dog-ear each book based on how many pages I have to read to finish that book each month. So, Monday is my faith-based book, Tuesday is psychology, Wednesday is leadership, Thursday is business, and Friday is Innovation/Creativity. I read my section for the day and catch up on the weekends if I don't get through it. That is the system that I have been using for over ten years now. Do I always hit it…no. Do I beat myself up for it…no. Do I keep going no matter what…yes! Do I read over 60 books a year this way…yes!

Now, don't be intimidated or overwhelmed by my system…it's what works for me. Many people hate reading more than one book at a time…great, do what works for you. The type of system isn't as important as simply just having a system.

So, what system can you create to keep you disciplined and focused? Whatever you do, you need to make a real systemized habit that keeps you growing and consuming resources to maximize your potential. Start small and work your way up over time. I didn't start with the system I currently have; that took me years of creating small disciplines that led to my current habit.

LESSON #4: LIVE OUT WHAT
YOU LEARN ABOUT

Most people are educated way beyond their level of effectiveness. They know a lot but do very little. Our level of effectiveness is not about knowing more… it's about doing more. Famous motivational speaker and author Jim Rohn said, "Don't let your learning lead to knowledge. Let your learning lead to action." The goal of education is transformation. When we take what we learn and live it out, our future transforms for the better. Many people have consumed a vast amount of resources but have nothing to show for it. Don't let this be your experience. Make sure your learning is leading to action.

Let's unpack how you can live out what you are learning about.

Write It Down

There is an old saying, "It's not real until it's written." I think our learning operates from a similar pattern. There is something powerful and memorable about untangling your thoughts by writing them down. For me, I have a notebook for each of the five categories I talked about in Lesson #1. As I read my chosen book for the day (Lesson #2), I underline things that stick out to me and then transfer those markings into my growth notebook. This system allows me to catalog the best ideas meaningful to me during my reading time.

However you want to do it, make sure you are writing down the things you are learning about. Many people will journal their ideas or write down a summary of what they just learned about. Whatever you do, make sure there is a transfer from reading/listening/watching whatever resource you are taking in to the written form.

Challenge Yourself

If you don't challenge yourself to do something with what you're learning about, you'll likely forget it. Turn your learning into something you challenge yourself to act on. Again, it's not just about knowledge; it's about action. So, at the end of your learning moment, ask yourself, "What will I do with what I just learned?" This question forces you to devise a creative way to practice something new. You may need to implement a new mindset, a new productivity tip, a new process, or a new perspective. Make sure that you change something in your behavior from what you learned.

Share It With Others

Our learning can't just be for us, especially as leaders. We must ensure we are passing on great ideas that will help others. Not only will you potentially impact someone else, but sharing what you're learning about it will help you retain it. In fact, cognitive studies have shown that teaching others gives us a 90% retention rate. It's the highest form of learning we can utilize.

The more you share what you are learning, the better you can process and understand it. It forces you to wrap your mind around the concept whenever you can communicate it. As leaders, we must develop those around us and share great resources and ideas to expedite the process.

3

Know Your Personality

Your personality is one of the most significant determiners of your behavior. It makes you unique and influences your thinking, feeling, and acting. Studies have shown that awareness of your personality can predict job satisfaction, academic success, and even how well you'll get along with others. No wonder personality is such a big topic of interest for psychologists and leaders.

So, what exactly is personality?

Personality is a complex and multi-faceted thing. It's made up of many different factors, including your values, beliefs, experiences, and ultimately your unique wiring from birth. All of these things come together to influence your behavior. As a result, personality can strongly predict how you'll behave in any given situation. For example, if your personality type is shy and withdrawn, you will likely avoid social situations.

Conversely, you're more likely to seek opportunities to socialize if you're outgoing and extroverted. Personality also plays a major role in coping with stress and handling difficult situations. For example, you're more likely to bounce back from setbacks if you're naturally optimistic and have a strong sense of self-efficacy. On the other hand, if you tend to be pessimistic and have low self-confidence, you're more likely to dwell on your failures and have a more challenging time moving on. Understanding your personality can help you better understand why you act the way you do and make it easier to change your future possibilities.

The concept of personality temperaments has been around since 400 BC. Hippocrates, a Greek physician who is considered the "father of medicine," was one of the first to study how our behaviors are fundamentally influenced. Hippocrates developed a personality typology in ancient Greece based on four temperaments: sanguine, choleric, melancholic, and phlegmatic. Each temperament was associated with a different set of physical and psychological characteristics. Hippocrates' personality theory was based on the belief that bodily fluids determine personality. By examining these various fluids, he believed that it was possible to understand a person's personality. Most of our modern-day personality assessments derive from this movement in history.

It is vital for you to know your personality. If there is one person you should become an expert on...it is yourself. Self-awareness is key to success. In fact, all success is built upon the foundation of knowing your unique personality.

Several personality assessments are available, such as Enneagram, Myers-Briggs, and Predictive Index, but my all-time favorite one I use for clients is DISC. DISC is a simple yet highly accurate tool and one of the leading personality profiles. It breaks down your unique personality into a blend of the four different temperaments.

D = Dominant
I = Inspiring
S = Steady
C = Contemplative

Each letter comes with a world of characteristics to accompany them. DISC will give you an easy and digestible framework for knowing who you are and how others operate. If you go to www.johnbarrettleadership.com/disc you can take an assessment to find out your unique personality blend. Your assessment will also contain a detailed breakdown of practical tips on how to utilize your personality to your fullest potential.

The more aware you are of yourself, the more you can lead yourself effectively. You can know what strengths to capitalize on and what weaknesses to work around.

Here is what personality can help you with:

PREDICTING YOUR FUTURE

Knowing your personality leads to understanding how you'll act in any given situation. The better you understand yourself, the better you can know what environments and situations you respond to best. Highly successful people know who they are;

therefore, they surround themselves with opportunities that will bring about the best in them. They go out of their way to fill their schedule with events, projects, and tasks that they know will cause them to behave in their strength zone. Likewise, knowing who you are gives you incredible insight into how you'll respond, allowing you to be intentional about your future.

I always try to anticipate every event, meeting, or interaction I will have when I start each day and coach myself to operate healthily. Knowing who I will meet with and what I'll encounter allows me to prepare for success as much as possible.

REFERENCING YOUR PAST

Hindsight is truly 20/20, especially for those who know their personality type. In fact, having great hindsight leads to great foresight. The better you understand your past behaviors, the more you learn about yourself. And the more you learn about yourself, the better equipped you are to predict your behavior. Unfortunately, most people don't take the necessary time to reflect on the past, thus causing them to keep repeating it rather than moving forward. Personality profiles resource you with understanding why past relationships and situations turned out the way they did.

The past is always the key to the future. What you learn from yesterday equips you with what you need today and propels you forward for a successful tomorrow.

GUIDING YOUR PRESENT

How can you know what to work on if you don't understand why you act the way you do? The more insight into your personality, the better you can recognize areas of improvement. You can understand why you are weak in some areas and strong in others, thus allowing you to tailor your growth. Just like a doctor diagnoses a patient so they can treat their issues, understanding our personality helps us analyze our issues. It's easier to improve yourself if you know why you are the way you are. If you want to shape your life in a way that causes you to be well-rounded, you'll need to study yourself so you can master yourself.

Knowing who you are can help temper your responses at the moment. When you start to see the unhealthy side of your personality trait rise, you can adjust because you know what is happening. Instead of being led by your unhealthy reactions, you can lead your reactions in a healthy expression.

(4)

Define
Your
Definition

There will always be more to do and not enough time to get it all done. The sooner you accept this truth, the sooner you can relax.

I coach many leaders who are always going, going, going but are never satisfied. The reason is that success is like a moving target. The moment you think you've arrived is the moment it moves further away. This is not a bad thing; it's what keeps us moving forward and stretching for more. But if not handled correctly it can drive a person mad feeling like they're chasing infinity.

You don't want to get caught up in the vortex of success. It will make you feel as though you're never good enough, never far enough, never anything enough. We all want to be successful, but we have to be careful that we don't become obsessed with it. Success can suck the life out of you if you don't balance it. The drive for more can drive you crazy.

So how do we keep from getting caught in the vortex of success?

Define What Success Is For You

If you haven't defined what success is for you how would you ever know if you've attained it? The answer; you wouldn't know if you were successful, and you just might miss the fact that you are. The most successful people have clearly defined what success is for them. They are not ignorant of what it is they are trying to accomplish. It is a clear target that is meaningful to them. They know what they are doing in order to get to where they want to go. After all, we don't want to get to a destination only to find out it isn't what we wanted.

> "The most successful people have clearly defined what success is for them."

Though you may have varying definitions of success for different areas of your life, the five things they should all have in common is: that it must be simple, specific, strategic, scalable, and significant.

Here are some things to think about as you define what success is:

IT MUST BE SIMPLE

Success can't be complicated. It should be easily defined. Clare Boothe Luce, one of the first women to serve in the U.S. Congress, famously told President John F. Kennedy, "A great man is one sentence." One day when you're gone, your life will be summed up in a few words. The good news is you get to choose what those words will be about.

You have the opportunity to define what success is for you now. Don't overcomplicate the process. Clarity is accomplished by keeping things easily memorable. Keep it short and to the point. Albert Einstein said this about complexities, "If you can't explain it to a six-year-old, you don't understand it yourself." Your definition of success must be clearly recognized when you've achieved it.

IT MUST BE SPECIFIC

Success must be specifically measurable. It has to have a quantifiable outcome. To say that your definition for financial success is to be wealthier, doesn't cut it. It needs to be more like this example: To be debt free, with an annual income of $x, and giving x% to charity.

You must be able to know if you are living successfully. Saying you want to be wealthier, is like chasing infinity, how would you know if you caught it? The more specific you are, the better equipped you'll be to make it happen. It's incredible what activates inside of you when your mind locks on a particular target. Author Napoleon Hill said, "When your desires are strong enough, you will appear to possess superhuman powers to achieve."

IT MUST BE STRATEGIC

Success has to be an intentional endeavor. We can't treat success like little Johnny did. One day, little Johnny got his bow and arrows out to work on his target practice. He pulled arrows out of his quiver one by one and proceeded to shoot in every direction he felt like. He then would walk up to wherever the arrow had landed and draw a target right around it, making it a bull's eye every time. Several arrows and targets later, his sister said, "You don't do target practice that way. You draw the target, then shoot the arrow." Johnny responded: "I know that, but if you do it my way, you never miss!"

Unlike little Johnny, we can't just let our life go any direction it takes us and then draw a target around wherever we end up and call it a success. We need to be maximizing our potential by creating the success we desire. We have to be intentional about what our lives are about. Don't just throw random numbers, ideas, and metrics without knowing why you want to reach them. Many people throw arbitrary ideas out when defining success, but in order to make it count, be strategic about everything.

IT MUST BE SCALABLE

Yes, success must be attainable and practical, but it should also stretch you to scale higher than you've ever been. Success has to be something that challenges you to elevate. It must cause you to reach further than you've ever reached, and dream bigger than you've ever dreamt. In fact, if your dreams don't scare you, you're probably not dreaming big enough. Your definition should stretch you to greater heights. Artist Michelangelo said, "The greatest danger for most of us is not that our aim is too high and we miss it, but that it is too low and we reach it." Your definition of success should be just out of reach of what you currently can do, so it causes you to scale up to a higher level. Never belittle your dreams because of an inner fear that tells you it's too much. Dare to believe in yourself.

IT MUST BE SIGNIFICANT

Success must embody a worthy cause. At the end of our life, we will have wanted to make a significant impact in the world. We will have wanted to know our life mattered somehow, some-way. There was an old country song written years ago called Live Like You Were Dying. In it, county music star Tim Mc-Graw encouraged us to live life to the fullest with no regrets. It received many accolades, including a Grammy Award for Song of the Year. Regardless if you liked the song or not, it had a powerful message.

We all need to awaken the desire inside of us to make every day count. We must know that our effort is successful in order to live life to the fullest. The only way for us to know this is to make our definition of success deserving of a significant impact. Make sure you leave a legacy because of the difference you desire to make. Only living for yourself is a very lonely life. Henry Ford said, "A business that makes nothing but money is a poor business."

Take some time to sit down and craft your definitions of success for each area of your life. Don't rush through it, but be methodical about it. The first step to being highly successful is to know what it is you are trying to do.

5

Be Mentally Strong

There has been a lot of discussion around mental health these days. Fortunately, we have recognized the need to keep our minds in good standing. But even with all the mental health days off, seminars, and HR resources people have been given most aren't getting any better at being mentally stronger. It's not enough to take a mental health day off of work without learning how to become a mentally strong person. In fact, the more mentally strong you become, the less you'll have to escape to get better. Mental toughness works like a muscle, the more you work it, the stronger it gets.

The battlefield of success takes first takes place in the mind. You cannot manifest an outward reality that is inconsistent with your inner reality...or maybe, I should say, you can, but, it will come crashing down eventually. The dissonance between the two realities will cause an internal earthquake with maximum damage.

Successful people are always mentally strong individuals. That's not to say they don't have challenges. Remember, I said the battlefield is in the mind. We all battle the negative, pessimistic, and fearful inner self that tries to sabotage our success. It's not that successful people don't have problems, they just don't allow their problems to have them.

The mentally stronger you are the greater your chances of success. This is a universal reality that determines how successful you are in your relationships, your job, your finances, your health, your fulfillment...basically everything!

Here's how to be mentally strong:

BE OPTIMISTIC

Negative people live unhealthy lives. Their relationships suffer, their work suffers, their productivity suffers, and their happiness suffers. We all know we shouldn't be negative, but negativity is a sneaky thing. You won't even realize you are being negative, because negativity disguises itself in realism. Instead of saying you're negative, you'll say you're just being real. Don't make agreements with negative thinking, it only destroys hope and success. Director and screenwriter, David Lynch said, "Negativity is the enemy of creativity." I couldn't agree more. Just remember any thought that focuses on the problem and not the opportunity is negative! When you change your view from obstacles to opportunities you'll begin to see solutions. Negative people only see problems, while successful people see potential. What appears to be a setback can actually be a setup for something amazing. Optimism always believes there is purpose hiding behind problems.

BE SLIPPERY

Your mind can either be sticky or slippery. This means things will either stick easily or slide off easily. The more slippery your mind is, the less of a chance unhealthy things have to stick. Mentally weak people have sticky thoughts. They allow hurtful words, unhealthy actions, and negative experiences to consume their mind, thus making no room for solutions and productivity. Mentally strong people have a slip n' slide mind; they allow things to easily be forgiven and forgotten. If you allow words, actions, and looks to be a dart on your board you eventually become broken. It's not that people aren't hurtful, they are at times, but that doesn't mean you have to let it stick in you. Understand that hurting people hurt people. There is almost always a reason why people respond negatively in situations. The moment you realize the bigger issue is not what was done, but why it was done is the moment you'll stop allowing things to stick so easily. The faster you can recover from "bad stuff" the greater your chances of success. Don't hold on to negative things in your life or they will consume you.

BE CONTROLLING

I don't mean controlling others but controlling yourself. Mentally strong people don't allow their environment to dictate their wellbeing, they let their wellbeing dictate their environment. Mentally strong people don't say things like, "I am just over this day and ready for it to end." That statement is an example of someone who is allowing circumstances to control their well-being. I know we ALL have bad days, and that's okay, but mental strength does what it has to in order to recover quickly. One of my favorite authors, James Allen said, "Man is made or unmade by himself. By the right choice he ascends. As a being of power, intelligence, and love, and the lord of his own thoughts, he holds the key to every situation." You can't control your circumstances, but you can always control your response to those circumstances, and mentally strong people strive for that. You have to take responsibility for your thoughts and responses. If you constantly blame others or circumstances for your problems it's a sure sign you haven't dealt with yourself. I am certainly not belittling very hard situations we have all gone through, and I am not making light of real mental trauma, but we can never move forward while we're blaming others. We have to keep our thoughts moving forward into a greater future rather than being stuck in the past.

6

Dress
For
Success

Believe it or not, what you wear determines how successful you'll become. Now I am not talking about only wearing expensive clothes, but rather wearing what makes you feel great! What you wear greatly affects your confidence thus affecting your productivity. And your productivity determines your success.

Wendy L. Patrick cites this study in her article Power Role Play: Dressing For Success Makes You Successful from Psychology Today.

> *One study (Adam and Galinsky, 2012) showed*
> *that participants who wore a white coat and*
> *identified it as a doctor's coat exhibited better*
> *sustained attention than participants wearing a*
> *white coat who identified it as just a coat, or as*

a painters coat. Another study (Van Stockum &
De Caro, 2014) showed that students who wore
a white lab coat demonstrated a higher degree
of attention to problem solving.

I experienced this phenomenon firsthand with a client of mine who is a doctor. As we worked through some of his challenges in his practice we actually identified one of the limiting factors was his attire. Over time he had stopped wearing his doctor's coat and it slowly eroded his confidence. By simply committing to dressing the part he began to improve his performance as a physician. This made an impact on his overall success of the practice.

Here are some tips to dress for success.

WEAR WHAT MAKES YOU FEEL CONFIDENT

The best leaders possess confidence in who they are and what they can accomplish. It's not a matter of ego, but healthy self-assurance. You're at your best when you feel at your best. Don't get too caught up in wearing what you're supposed to wear, but rather what you feel good in. Feeling good trumps looking good. With that said…wear appropriate clothes for the part you want to play. I don't just mean feeling good as in comfortable, but feeling good as in confident.

> **"You're at your best when you feel at your best."**

Probably not the best idea to wear sweatpants into a boardroom presentation, unless you are promoting fitness I guess!

The more uncomfortable we feel, the more we release high levels of cortisol in our body, which is the stress hormone. The more cortisol rises at the moment, the more confused and muddy our thinking becomes. This is why we forget simple things in fearful situations. For example, in a meeting with someone, we feel intimated by we begin to shrink down as cortisol rises and we find ourselves forgetting everything we wanted to say. When we leave the meeting we are frustrated with ourselves because we literally felt like we weren't present at all. When cortisol lowers back down after the meeting we now remember all the things we wanted to say and how we should have said it.

So in order to bring our best self to meetings and challenges we need to practice the art of opening up our body language and getting ourselves into a confident state of mind. Amy says, "Focus less on the impression you're making on others and more on the impression you're making on yourself." When your own self-image is strong you come across as confident and inspiring. This means you have to truly love yourself...I know sounds mushy...but it is VERY true. I don't mean love yourself in an arrogant way, but in a healthy self-confident way.

WEAR WHAT MATCHES YOUR PERSONALITY

Don't force what you wear. If it doesn't match your personality and persona don't wear it. It is vital that who you are at what you wear align. It's also important to know your signature attire. Everyone has a unique style to themselves, find out yours and capitalize on it. Steve Jobs was known for wearing his black turtle neck...everywhere. Mark Zuckerberg is known for his many t-shirts. Bill Gates seems to always sport a button-down, sweater, and jeans.

The moment you start comparing yourself to others is the moment you will begin to lose. There will always be someone further along than you and if you compare yourself to them the door to discouragement will open and you WILL walk through it. However, there are also those who are not as far along as you are and if you compare yourself to them you can easily start thinking you are better and allow arrogance to kill your creativity. The point...stop comparing your worth with others. Trust that what you have to offer is worth something. I see many people who miss out on a great life because they simply have lost their value.

Know who you are so you can dress for your success. Find your colors and utilize your style to your advantage.

WEAR WHAT MARKS WHERE
YOU WANT TO BE

Dress for the future. What I mean by that is knowing the person you want to one day become. Get a vision of who you want to be and dress accordingly. If you see yourself as a business professional dress to that style. If you see yourself as a personal trainer dress to that profession. Clothes will take your reputation somewhere, make sure it's where you want to go. Whatever it is you are serving to become make sure your wardrobe matches that future. Dress it and eventually, you'll become it.

If you really want to become something then you need to simply start acting like it now in order to become it later. You don't wake up one day and become who you've always wanted to be. Rather, you wake up one day and simply start being who you've always wanted to be so you'll eventually become who you've always wanted to be. Zig Ziglar said, "Before a person can achieve the kind of life he wants, he must think, act, talk, and conduct himself in all of his affairs as would the person he wishes to become." Every day is an audition for the person you want to become.

7

Expect
More
From
Yourself

It's said that one day, Frederick the Great of Prussia was walking on the outskirts of Berlin when he encountered a very old man walking ramrod-straight in the opposite direction.

"Who are you?" Frederick asked his subject.

"I am a king," replied the old man.

"A king!" laughed Frederick. "Over what kingdom do you reign?"

"Over myself," was the proud old man's reply.

Like the old man, we, too, must take responsibility for ourselves. We are the captain of our destiny, and no one else can do it for us. Businessman Ray Kroc said, "The quality of a leader is reflected in the standards they set for themselves." The most effective form of leadership is to exemplify the high expectations you set on others.

You are responsible for yourself. If others have to set a higher expectation on you than you set for yourself, you'd better rethink your future.

We don't see things as they are; we see things as we are. Self-expectations become a catalyst for growth or an inhibitor of growth. You will have difficulty reaching your fullest potential if you constantly degrade yourself. You will always be discouraged if you are continually thinking poorly of yourself. However, if you consistently believe in your resilience, you'll discover new opportunities. You'll use your strengths to build greater success if you consistently recognize them. Philosopher Lao Tzu said, "He who conquers others is strong; he who conquers himself is mighty."

If you really want to know how you're doing at expecting more from yourself, ask this revealing question...Would You Follow Yourself?

This question forces us to look within and be honest with ourselves truthfully. You have to be what you want to see in others. The actions of a team will always mirror the behaviors of the leader. The truth is simple...people do what people see.

I once heard a great parental statement: "Children seldom listen to their parents, but they never fail to imitate them." This statement makes complete sense, especially if you have kids and have experienced it...I know I have.

The other day, while my family and I were running errands, we got a call informing us that we would have some unexpected company within the hour. We all know "the call," don't we? Panic immediately sets in as thoughts of the morning's breakfast dishes piled in the sink, toys all over the living room floor, and toothpaste tubes left on bathroom counters enter our minds. We knew we needed to get home quickly and pick up the house. As we zoomed down the road, we gave our two daughters a motivating pep talk and specific tasks to get things cleaned quickly. I specifically told them to make sure they had a great attitude when they started to clean since we had a lot to do in a few minutes. I really stressed the "good attitude" part in my instructions! We got home and began to clean at warp speed. Our daughters did a great job. All was going well...and then my wife asked me to vacuum the living room...uh oh...vacuum? I thought that was a bit overboard, so I huffed and puffed and argued with her about why I had to be the one to vacuum. My daughters immediately caught on to my unwillingness to take on the task before me and simultaneously said, "Remember, Daddy, have a good attitude!" I was clearly not setting the right example for my girls, and they noticed...I was caught.

To be a great leader, you must learn to lead yourself first. I have found that the hardest person I have ever had to lead is none other than me. President Theodore Roosevelt once stated, "If I could kick the person responsible for all my troubles I wouldn't be able to sit down for a week." We cannot lead others well if we do not lead ourselves well. If we have trouble motivating ourselves, we will have a hard time motivating others. Great leaders push themselves further than anyone else ever will. Walt Disney was a dreamer and pushed himself even when others rejected his ideas. He was known for this motto: "Whatever you do, do it well. Do it so well that when people see you do it they will want to come back and see you do it again and they will want to bring others and show them how well you do what you do."

Lead from the front by modeling the behavior you desire to see. Ask yourself these questions,

"Would you follow yourself?"
"Would you be motivated by yourself?"
"Would you be filled with vision if you were following yourself?"

If the answer is yes, congratulations, you lead by example. If you answered no, you need to start challenging yourself to get out there and become the leader you need to be.

Remember these truths:

- To be an influential leader, you have to believe in your potential.
- You will never enjoy life to the fullest if you don't challenge yourself to be your best.
- You have to value yourself if you want to find value in what you do.
- You need to be your biggest fan, greatest motivator, and loudest cheerleader.
- If you don't value yourself, don't expect others to place a high value on you.
- Do not presume you'll get the most out of life if you don't get the most out of yourself.

- The most important opinion we have is the opinion we have of ourselves.
- How you see yourself is how you will see the world around you.
- You will never outperform the way you view yourself.
- You have to see value in who you are before you can add value to others.

Expect yourself to be a person of passion, purpose, and possibilities in all you do. You are created for more than you can imagine. You are designed to offer this world something extraordinary. And only you have the ability to take what you've been given and use it for good. So, never bury your potential because you've believed the lie that you are not important. Zig Ziglar said, "You were born to win, but to be a winner, you must plan to win, prepare to win, and expect to win.".

Get resources to help you grow as a leader. Get around people who will inspire you and mentor you. Get a leadership coach to help you be your best and lead others to be their best. You have to self-invest if you want to be the best. Set your expectations high, and you will rise to that level. Be the best version of yourself.

Make Your
FIFO
Greater Than Your
FOMO

FOMO is a buzzword that has recently appeared in our culture, meaning Fear Of Missing Out. Our society is plagued with people feeling like they are on the outside looking in. With everyone's highlight reel of their best moments on social media, others unnecessarily become discouraged by the realistic view of their own life. FOMO can cause you to make rash decisions at the moment. It causes a play now, pay later cycle of life.

Rather than suffering from FOMO, people need to be guided by, what I call, FIFO (Faith In Future Opportunities). Discipline activates when you believe there is something better in the future than what you experience in the present. People who have a strong sense of FIFO tend to pay now to play later. They see the future with optimism and hope. This outlook causes them to delay their instant gratification for future greatness. French poet Victor Hugo said, "The future has several names. For the weak, it is impossible. For the fainthearted, it is unknown, but for the valiant, it is ideal."

Throughout the 60s and 70s, Walter Mischel conducted experiments at Stanford University that became known as the Marshmallow Test. Children were put in a room by themselves with one single marshmallow. They were told they could either eat the marshmallow immediately or wait for an extended amount of time and receive more. Only 3 out of 10 children could instantly resist the urge to eat the marshmallow. What's fascinating is that 30 years after the study was completed, research was done to determine what happened to the test subjects later in life as adults. They found that the "Delayers" were predominately more successful in life overall. However, the "Non-Delayers" were 30% more likely to be overweight, suffer from drug addictions, and have a record of criminal activity.

Truly, something invigorating happens to us when we have patience and expectancy for the future. When there is a sense of hope for the future, there is a surge of power in the present. Those whose FIFO is greater than their FOMO will increase their discipline to be more successful down the road.

Every person sees the future through one of two lenses. These lenses determine how one approaches their decisions. Here are the two lenses:

- Scarcity – the belief that there is a short supply
- Abundance – the belief that there is more than enough

Your outlook will determine your opportunities. I have yet to meet someone thriving into the future with a scarcity mindset. Although, I commonly meet people stuck in their challenges that exude scarcity.

Behavior is an overflow of belief. The moment you believe the future is scarce is the moment you'll lose motivation to get there. However, the moment you believe the future is abundant is the moment you'll begin to create the drive that will lead you to greater success. The future belongs to the abundantly optimistic, while the present is inundated with the scarcest pessimists. Scarcity keeps you weighted down in apathy, while abundance keeps you soaring in enthusiasm. The great poet Ralph Waldo Emerson said, "Enthusiasm is one of the most powerful engines of success. When you do a thing, do it with all your might. Put your whole soul into it. Stamp it with your own personality. Be active, be energetic, be enthusiastic and faithful, and you will accomplish your object. Nothing great was ever achieved without enthusiasm."

Here's how to become more abundantly optimistic:

SEE SETBACKS AS SETUPS

Challenges are just stepping stones to growth. When you change your view from obstacles to opportunities, you'll begin to see solutions. Negative people only see problems, while successful people see potential. What appears to be a setback can actually be a setup for something extraordinary. Abundance always believes there is purpose hiding behind problems.

SEE LESS AS MORE

Don't be afraid of loss. In fact, sometimes, the only way to add is by subtracting. Those that fear losing and having less are trapped in their fear. My mentor John C. Maxwell taught me early on that you have to give up in order to go up. If you want to go higher, you have to be willing to let some things go. Scarcity always tries to hold on and never let go of what you've got. But abundance is ready to let go of what you've got in order to get what you ain't got! Less is more if you believe in an abundant future.

SEE WHAT COULD BE AS WHAT IS

Too many people wait until they've got something before they do something. They wait for title and position before they lead with influence and confidence. They wait to have lots of money before they start investing with what they've got. They wait for others to befriend them before opening up and being friends. Basically, too many people are putting off living life until they "arrive." The problem is you don't get to a greater future until you start living like it now. I always say, "Every day is an audition for the person you want to become." See what could be and live like it is. Then you will begin to live more abundantly.

SEE GRATITUDE AS AN ATTITUDE

Difficulties are inevitable, but complaining is optional. I've heard it said that some people don't just complain occasionally; they complain recreationally. We all know people who are tethered to negativity. The problem is that negativity and ungratefulness result in faithlessness. You can't be your best while living in negativity. Some people miss out on being blessed because they are too busy being stressed. Gratitude brings joy to our life. Happiness is based on what is around us, but joy is based on what is within us. When you are genuinely grateful inside, you can move into FIFO with whatever happens on the outside.

I came across this great poem that puts gratitude in perspective.

I am thankful for the mess to clean up after a party because it means friends have surrounded me.

I am thankful for the income taxes I pay because it means that I'm employed.

I am thankful for the clothes that fit a little too snug because it means I have enough to eat.

I am thankful for the spot I find at the far end of the parking lot because it means I am capable of walking.

I am thankful for all the complaining I hear about our government because it means we have freedom of speech.

I am thankful for the lady in the next row who sings off key because it means that I can hear.

I am thankful for the piles of laundry because it means my loved ones are nearby.

I am thankful for the lawn that needs mowing, windows that need cleaning, and gutters that need fixing because it means I have a home.

I am thankful for my huge heating bill because it means that I am warm.

I am thankful for weariness and aching muscles at the end of the day because it means that I have been productive.

I am thankful for the alarm that goes off in the early morning hours because it means that I am alive.

9

Talk
To
Yourself

Words are not only powerful, but they're prophetic as well. They can become a self-fulfilling prophecy of our future.

We all have conversations with ourselves in our minds. I would argue that the most important conversation we daily have is the one with ourselves. There is no one you spend more time with than yourself. You are internally commentating on every experience you have throughout your entire day. You get no break, no rest, no silence from yourself. You follow yourself around every day at every moment. And guess what? You have an opinion about your every move and every thought you have. There is no human voice louder than the one in our own head.

Make no mistake, the person who has the most influence on you...is yourself. This is why self-talk determines self-worth. The words you say to yourself will ultimately define who you'll become. The good news is that you can talk your way into a better future.

This isn't just positive mumbo-jumbo hype; this is how we were created. The brain comprises billions of pathways where information travels through at all moments. These pathways are constantly under construction in a term referred to as Neuroplasticity. Your brain is ever-adapting and reinventing itself based on its receiving information. As new pathways are used, old ones begin breaking down.

This process can be good news or terrible news, depending on what information your brain is currently processing. Environment, experiences, emotions, thoughts, and words have a tremendous impact on our ability to function optimally. What you consistently put into your brain is what begins to form in habitual pathways of activity. This is why we can learn new skills as we continuously practice them. Our old path of confusion and chaos begins to break down as we chart a new course of developing the skill. The nature of what you think about and what you say to yourself will literally rewire your brain.

Thus, your thoughts and words will become your new actions and habits over time. What you are communicating to yourself will wire your brain to produce an easy pathway to that result. If you constantly say and believe you aren't a creative person, you will actually create that behavior. Your brain will have a hard time being creative because it will flow to the unimaginative pathway you have constructed. If you consistently say you don't have enough resources to get something done, your brain will have difficulty finding the resources to get something done.

This limiting self-talk is why we hit mental roadblocks when doing something we've never done; our brains are trying hard to construct new pathways. If we give up and surrender to the pressure of negativity, we will stop constructing innovative pathways and start constructing impossibility pathways.

Three aspects of talking to yourself can set you up for success: What you say, how you say it, and when you say it.

Let's break these down.

WHAT YOU SAY

Your daily conversation will either be an encouragement or a discouragement to yourself; it's your choice. I have personally found that I am my worst enemy or best friend, depending on the situation. The person who controls my well-being is me. Consequently, I have the most challenging time with myself more than anyone else. What I say to myself determines how well I do. You can't speak failure over your life and expect to live successfully. You'll become what you tell yourself you are. Keep saying you're a loser, and sure enough, you'll live out that experience. Keep saying you're a winner and watch how you'll start to win in life. What you talk about, you tend to get more of. Keep your self-narrative meticulously positive, and I promise you'll see unbelievable results.

HOW YOU SAY IT

Columbia University professor of psychology Ethan Kross studied how using different pronouns in your self-talk affects your performance. He formed two groups of people who were told they had to give a speech to a large group of people with only five minutes of preparation. On top of the high-stress situation, he stated that this large group of people listening would be speech experts judging them and that their presentation would also be videotaped.

Both groups were told that positive self-talk would alleviate their stress and help their chances of being better communicators. One group was instructed to refer to themselves in first-person using the word "I" in their self-talk. The other group was instructed to refer to themselves in the second or third person, using their name or the word "you." Kross' study found that the second group who used second-person and third-person self-talk were considerably less stressed and performed significantly better in their presentations. "We find that a subtle linguistic shift—shifting from 'I' to your own name—can have really powerful self-regulatory effects," Kross told NPR. "It's almost like you are duping yourself into thinking about you as though you were another person," Kross said.

You need to talk to yourself just as you would another person. Use your specific name to refer to yourself, which will boost your confidence. Using your name allows you to separate yourself from the challenges around you. It lifts you to a high vantage point above your situation. Speak to yourself as though you are already the person you desire to become.

WHEN YOU SAY IT

Everyone deals with negative self-talk, especially when they are getting ready to do something outside their comfort zone. In fact, you'll always hear the gremlin inside start to chatter when you are pushing yourself further than you've ever pushed. That negative voice will tell you that you can't do it, it won't work, or who do you think you are. It will try and limit you from your destiny. You have to understand that when you get ready to do something big, negative self-talk will always whisper its screeching voice. You have to combat that voice with a greater voice–a voice of confidence and courage. The moment you hear the gremlin inside is when your inner warrior has to shout louder. It's a fight. A battle that will determine if you'll step out.

Know that you'll need to build yourself up when it is the hardest. Everything in you may want to tear yourself down, but you have to stand your ground. Expect this ugly voice to speak up as soon as you start to think bigger and crush its power with a shout of boldness within. Never let the ugly voice inside of you keep you from the great things in front of you.

10

Get
Selfish

I learned an unexpected life lesson during my experience the first time I flew as a child. I'll never forget the stewardess going through the whole pre-flight safety presentation. It terrified me. Not only was I already scared to be flying before I even got to the airport, but her instructions about what to do in case of emergency sent me to a whole nutha level of fear. I envisioned the plane tearing in half as I fought for my life...not too pleasant for anyone, especially a kid. But I'll never forget how emphatic she ensured we all put on our oxygen masks before helping anyone else get theirs on. She stated, "You can't help others to safety if you are not safe first."

That line has stuck out to me throughout my life.

Taking time for yourself is essential if you want to be successful. Unfortunately, you have to get selfish to achieve a healthy quality of life. Always giving without receiving eventually leads to burnout. Today, most people's life ratios look like 9:1 output, leaving a 1:9 input.

You can only output what you have inputted. You cannot give what you do not have. Productivity shuts down when you have not inputted enough for it to overflow out of you. It is not that you are uninspired, lazy, indecisive, or even stuck; you simply have not filled your energy tank with enough juice. When you input time for rest and rejuvenation, you will output greater stamina. Productivity is an overflow of what we have put inside us.

Always outputting and never inputting will be your ultimate downfall. Relationships will suffer, productivity will suffer, health will suffer, and you will suffer from not having a well-balanced life. We need to shoot more for a 1:1 ratio of output and input, meaning you need to refuel your tank every time you extract a large amount of energy. If you study some of the most successful people, you will find they have created vast amounts of margin in their schedule to recover and replenish their energy. Still, for some reason, we believe the lie that, to be productive and successful, you must work 65+ hours a week. Reject that myth and make sure you are scheduling in margin along with all of your other responsibilities.

You must be mentally and physically prepared for the opportunities that come your way, and margin is the way to allow for this. Margin is the white space in our lives and on our calendars: the time we set aside for rest, creativity, and quiet. Living with no margin leads to burnout. Is your schedule over-filled? It's time to take something(s) off your plate. It's impossible to manage life without margin; you have to figure out what to release to make room for white space, which is as essential as any other scheduled item. Remember, for every one thing you add to your schedule, you need to subtract another thing. Likewise, for every yes, there should also be a no. Identifying what is truly important in life is the key to deciding what remains and what goes.

Are you going to bed too late, waking up too early, racing out the door, always running behind schedule? You can't stay on top of things when you are always playing catch-up. Be intentional about scheduling breaks between meetings and downtime throughout your week. Make space for your imagination to expand through creative endeavors.

An old milk commercial stated: Happy cows produce happy milk. This commercial was based on scientific research proving happier cows produce more nutritious milk. In a study published in the Journal of Endocrinology, researchers from the University of Wisconsin, Madison, found that cows exposed to Serotonin (a natural chemical known to boost happiness) produced milk with an increased calcium level.

The truth is our emotional state can make or break our ability to succeed. When we are in an increased state of happiness, our brain gets greater blood flow, thus allowing us to think better. However, when we are in distress, our mind becomes very clouded as we try to think. Feeling stress has been shown to decrease activity in your cerebellum, which slows the brain's ability to process new information. This significantly limits your ability to engage in creative problem-solving. Our thoughts have the power to suppress or release neurochemicals that determine our happiness.

When we are in an increased state of happiness, our brain gets greater blood flow, thus allowing us to be more productive.

The good news is that we can think our way into success. What I mean by this is that choosing to be optimistic, positive, and hopeful releases the neurochemical Serotonin in our body, thus increasing our ability to be happy and productive. Shawn Achor, the author of The Happiness Advantage, wrote, "When we are happy—when our mindset and mood are positive—we are smarter, more motivated, and thus more successful. Happiness is the center, and success revolves around it."

If you are going to unleash your potential, you have to intentionally create a life you enjoy. I love how author Seth Godin said, "Instead of wondering when your next vacation is, maybe you should set up a life you don't need to escape from."

(11)

Fail
With
Excitement

You Failed

The two most feared combination of words throughout school. In fact, I can remember having reoccurring nightmares after graduating high school that I failed my classes and would never get out. These dreams haunted me for a few years even though I was done with grade school. Thankfully I recovered and can say I am nightmare-free!

Growing up, we are taught that failure is a very very bad thing. It is something to avoid at all costs. The greatest thing a young person fears is failure. Unfortunately, that fear follows us into adulthood as well. But fearing failure only limits our potential. I believed that all failure led to the dark side...but I was wrong.

Failure has two sides to it. On one side it can be dark and does lead to destruction. But the other side of it is productive and leads to a great lesson. Depending on which side you land on will determine what happens next. The good news is that you get to decide which side of failure you operate from.

The only way you truly fail is to not learn from your failure. Failure in and of itself is what it is; it's what you do with it that makes you or breaks you. Failure doesn't make you a failure unless you allow it to defeat you. But when you allow your failure to be your teacher you'll grow stronger from it. Failure doesn't define you, it refines you. Without failure how would we ever know what not to do? A person who succeeds without failure is a myth. It doesn't happen…at least not true success. Robert Kennedy said, "Only those who dare to fail greatly can ever achieve greatly."

Childhood behavioral studies have shown us that a child only learns to walk when they have failed to walk. Without the failure of falling, they will never learn how to gain their balance. Now, we could try to keep them from failure and tell a child over and over how muscle dexterity works, how to move the kneecap in the proper direction, etc… but that would not make sense to them. A child learns to walk because they are learning how not to walk. After many lessons on how not to walk, they eventually begin to understand how to walk. It is in their failure that they learn how to succeed.

Here are 5 ways to respond to your failures:

FAIL HUMBLY

Don't hide, fight, or avoid failure. The moment you think you're too good not to fail is the moment you set yourself up for disaster. Be humble when you fail. Admit your mistakes and shortcomings. Being honest with yourself and others is ok. If you can't fail humbly, you won't succeed humbly. Entitlement and greed overtake those who think they are better than they are. Humility unlocks the door to growth.

Stop trying to live without failure

FAIL QUICKLY

Better to fail small and fast than to avoid it and fail later when the stakes are higher. The faster you

> **"The faster you learn, the faster you can advance."**

learn, the faster you can advance. And remember failure is a much better teacher than success. Don't wait too long to get going in what you feel you need to do. Fearing failure causes paralysis. It keeps us from stepping out with courage. Better to learn as you go than to get so far down the road you have to go back and relearn what you never learned from the beginning.

FAIL CURIOUSLY

Don't get caught up in the emotion of failure. Be unaffectedly curious as you fail. Emotional debris can cloud your judgment in the midst of challenges. You have to remove your emotional attachment to the failure and objectively look at why the failure happened.

Deal with yourself before you deal with your failure. Curiosity causes you to lean in and learn why whatever you did didn't work. If you are angry, bitter, hurt, embarrassed, or skewed you'll miss the lesson. Keep curiosity at the forefront of all that you do and you'll become better as a result.

FAIL FORWARDLY

Whenever you fail and take the time to reflect as to why you failed you'll learn a lesson. But it's not enough just to learn the lesson you then have to apply what you've learned in order to move forward. Failure should propel you forward eventually. It may initially be two steps back, but when done right will catapult you five steps forward. It's how you apply what you've learned that will make the difference. Failing does nothing beneficial unless you intentionally change something as a result of it. Keep doing what you've always done and you'll always get what you've always got. In order to change the outcome, you have to change something in the variables.

FAIL CONTINUOUSLY

Most people assume success is a predetermined calculated formula, but rather it is more likely that someone tried something and it happened to work. For some reason, we have a mythical and somewhat magical thought that those who have attained success did so with a clear plan they never deviated from. But success rarely happens this way. It is usually the result of trial and error. And after many attempts, something actually broke through. Start to tinker around with new ideas, new systems, and new opportunities. Begin to think outside the box that you've always thought in. Don't be afraid to fail as you venture out into new territory. Play the long game of success.

Change your outlook on failure and you'll open up a whole new level of learning. Never fear failure, embrace it in order to become the best you can be. Your future will be dependent upon your ability to fail, learn from it, and get back up stronger than you were before. Henry Ford said, "Failure is simply the opportunity to begin again, this time more intelligently."

12

Be Resolute
In
Your
Pursuit

Have you ever had a really terrible day?

One of those days where everything that can go wrong does go wrong? Read this true story about a guy who had a challenging day, to say the least...

Bryan Heiss lived in Provo, Utah. One day in 1982, he awoke to find a leak in the ceiling of his apartment. The water was dripping in his face, so he jumped out of bed and called his landlord to see what could be done about the problem. When he stood up, he splashed in the water that was already gathering on the carpet. His landlord told him to rent a water vacuum quickly.

Bryan tore down the flight of stairs to get in his car to rent a wet vac, but he discovered that all four tires on his car were flat. He went back upstairs, reached for the phone, and was shocked so severely it nearly knocked him down. Bryan then shouted for a friend and asked him to take him to get help.

When he got back downstairs, Bryan found that someone had stolen his car. He knew it didn't have much gas, so he and his friend walked a few blocks, found the car, pushed it to a service station, and put gas in the tank and air in the tires.

Bryan later returned home and went upstairs to get dressed for an ROTC graduation ceremony he had scheduled that night. He donned his uniform and tried to get out of the house, but the water had caused the door to swell in its frame. He had to scream until someone could come and kick in the door from the outside.

When he finally jumped in his car, he immediately realized that he'd sat on his bayonet, which he had carelessly left in the driver's seat. Bryan was taken to the hospital for some very strategic surgery.

Let's pause for a second. You'd think that would be a good place to end this story, right? At this point, I just want to say, "And Bryan spent the night at the hospital and got a fresh start the next day," but that's not the end of this poor dude's day.

Friends took him home, and when Bryan opened the door, he saw that falling plaster had toppled the cage of his prized pet canaries, killing all of them. As he ran to the birds, across the wet carpet, he slipped. He hurt his back so badly he had to be taken to the hospital…again.

By this time a newspaper reporter caught up with Bryan and asked, "Mr. Heiss, how can you explain all of this happening to one person in a single day?" Bryan answered, "It looked like God was trying to kill me, but He kept missing."

We have all had bad days. The truth is you can't choose what happens to you but you can always choose what happens in you. No one can choose your attitude for you, that only comes from within. When crazy things happen to us we have a choice to make. We can choose to get BETTER or we choose to get BITTER. Our attitude will determine how we deal with the future.

Bad attitudes = a worse future
Good attitudes = a better future

Your attitude can change everything. It is not that everything will turn out perfect in your life with a good attitude it just means you choose to look at the good. This is why coach John Wooden would always say, "Things turn out best for those who make the best of the way things turn out." Winston Churchill said, "Attitude is a little thing that makes a big difference." Attitude can change a…

MESS into a MESSAGE
TEST into a TESTIMONY
VICTIM into a VICTORY

Attitude says a lot about what is inside of us. Show me a leader with a great attitude and I will show you leader who will do great things. Show me a leader with a bad attitude and I will show you a leader who will always struggle. Attitude is an inward feeling expressed by an outward behavior. You see, whatever is in us will eventually come out of us. Attitude is like the rudder of our life that guides us. So goes our attitude so goes our outlook on life. If we choose a great attitude life gets easier, however, when we choose a bad attitude life just gets harder. We can't change what happens to us, but we can choose how we handle it. Life is 10% what happens to us and 90% how we respond to it. American Novelist Raymond Chandler said, "Ability is what you're capable of doing. Motivation determines what you do. Attitude determines how well you do it."

The difference between successful people and unsuccessful people is their RESPONSE to circumstances. Successful people learn and live from their experiences. Unsuccessful people become bitter and give up because of their experiences. Unsuccessful people are REACTIVE, successful people are PROACTIVE. Proactive people take responsibility for their attitudes, reactive people are controlled by their attitudes. Unless you are able to harness your attitude you will never be able to steer your future in the right direction.

> **"The difference between successful people and unsuccessful people is their RESPONSE to circumstances."**

Reactive people get knocked off course easily. They are swayed by the way other people treat them, they become bitter about circumstances in their life as they feel insecure and out of control. Proactive people are focused on their journey, they get better as they learn from their circumstances, and they feel confident in their future!

In order to lead yourself, you need to live with resolve. Be the kind of person who gets stuff done. Anyone can start something, but it's those who can finish a task that become successful. The first mile of a marathon is crowded, but those who make it to the last mile have a wide-open path to the finish line. Seeing things through to completion is a sign of strong leadership. Author Jeff Goins said, "Don't waste your time with writing resolutions this New Year. Instead, focus on something else: resolve. While the words are similar, the difference in meaning is significant. A resolution is something you make. Resolve is something you have. In other words, commit. Choose into a process, not a set of audacious goals you'll never meet."

Fear conditions us to jump ship at the first sign of discomfort. In fact, the word fear comes from the Old English word *faer*, meaning "sudden ambush or attack." That is exactly what fear does: it attacks our courage and causes us to shrink back from following through.

You will never rise up to your potential unless you resolve to push through your fears. The moment we give in to our fears is the moment we cease growing. All true progress takes place just beyond the borders of fear. Successful people don't run from fear; they run through it. They gain courage by facing their fears head-on.

The path of potential runs straight through the heart of fear. You can't achieve your purpose without breaking through the fear barrier. Sadly, most people never meet their potential because they turn back or take a detour away from fear. They never experience the satisfaction of facing their fears and achieving

their goals, which leads to lives of complacency, or worse, re-
gret. Beast Mode Leaders are resolute in their pursuit.

(13)

Never Solve
Problems
Alone

To make things better, you have to become a great problem solver. Your influence grows as you provide solutions to problems. All business transactions are the result of someone paying to get a problem solved, whether meaningful or minuscule. The more you are able to provide solutions for people's problems, the more valuable you become to them. This ability requires that you bring unique ideas to the table. You can't just be a thermometer; you have to become a thermostat.

Thermometers read the temperature, but thermostats are able to change the temperature. Don't just bring problems to the table...offer solutions for them. No one wants to pay to find out they have a problem, but they will pay exceptionally well to get a problem fixed. Make it your practice never to bring a problem without a solution for it. Presenting a problem without a solution is really just a complaint in camouflage.

If you are struggling to find a solution, keep searching until you find one. Businessman J.P. Morgan said, "No problem can be solved until it is reduced to some simple form. The changing of a vague difficulty into a specific, concrete form is a very essential element in thinking." Don't give up on finding solutions; you may be moments away from a big breakthrough. Albert Einstein used to say, "It's not that I'm so smart, it's just that I stay with problems longer." It was his tenacity that enabled him to outlast his problems.

Solutions don't present themselves, they are sought after, hiding under conversations and thinking. The more options for solutions you can bring to problems, the more influential you become. People seek out those who can see fixes to problems.

> **"Solutions don't present themselves, they are sought after, hiding under conversations and thinking."**

If you surround yourself with small thinkers you will always find yourself surrounded with unsolvable problems. But when you surround yourself with big thinkers unsolvable problems become solvable. The problem didn't change, but your ability to think through them did.

If you want to break through challenges you have to have an inner circle that can help you. Lyndon B. Johnson said, "There are no problems we cannot solve together, and very few that we can solve by ourselves."

If you are facing a problem who do you go to? Who are the people that you surround yourself with that help you extract solutions?

Everyone should have someone that they can go to. If you don't have someone you can go to...your mission is to find that someone and develop the relationship. We were built for community. Your creative success will be dependent upon the people you surround yourself with. If you don't have a creative team to help you, you will limit your possibilities.

Collaboration breeds creativity.

Creative people have a tendency to act alone. They do well while working solo but have a hard time playing with others. It's not that they don't like other people, it's just that they feel others slow them down. Creative people don't like having to explain themselves and convince others about their ideas. They just want to do what they do without anything getting in their way. There is nothing wrong with wanting to move fast and avoid obstacles, but when we cut people out of the problem-solving process we end up cutting our effectiveness down as well. Creative people can create great things by themselves, but imagine how much more they could create with others. The truth is, that the more collaboration, the more creative we can be in the long run.

It's said that 2 Horses can pull about 9,000lbs. together. How much do you think 4 Horses can pull? You would assume 4 Horses are able to pull 18,000lbs. however, 4 Horses can pull over 30,000lbs. together. Teamwork doesn't double your effort, it multiplies your effort. There is a compound effect that occurs when creative collaboration takes place. If you truly want to multiply your impact you must work well with others. Going solo limits your potential. When you work alone you have to work 10x as hard to produce.

The key to solving problems together is to make sure you surround yourself with the right people. Let me share this formula when it comes to brainstorming with the right people…

WRONG IDEA + WRONG PERSON = DISASTER

If you have a wrong idea that is no good and you share it with the wrong person it may actually end up happening. And the result is an unsuccessful endeavor that was a waste of time. Make sure you share brainstorming time with the right kind of people who are the right fit for the solution. Seeking counsel from the wrong people gives you the wrong ideas. If the person is unqualified or uninterested in the process don't allow them to speak into the solution. Not everyone should be asked their opinion about specific matters.

RIGHT IDEA + WRONG PERSON = DEATH

Having a great idea that is shared with the wrong person can knock the wind out of your sails. Skeptical, non-dreaming, realist, unmotivated, no life, fearful, problem-finding, negative, purposeless people will bring death to great ideas. These people fight against every idea always picking out the bad. They kill ideas before they even have a chance to live. They're the kind of people who have a problem for every solution. Stay clear of people who habitually kill ideas with always pointing out the problems.

WRONG IDEA + RIGHT PERSON = PRACTICALITY

Sharing a wrong idea with the right person is wonderful. They are able to speak truth and practicality into the situation. You may have ideas that are just not very good. Having the right person who can help decipher the quality of an idea is a great thing that will enable progress. They will entertain the idea, but also help you work through better ideas. They will seek to build on your ideas not just tear them down. They tend to help you think through your wrong idea by asking great questions that get you to the right idea.

RIGHT IDEA + RIGHT PERSON = POSSIBILITIES

This is where the magic happens...when you have the right idea with the right person. This is where synergy and collaboration collide. This is where dreams are nurtured and built upon. Success lives in this equation. Always seek the right people with a track record of the right ideas in order to move quickly. Chemistry is necessary for collaboration. Seek out those whom you can work together with and spend time with them. Be proactive about meeting consistently with the right person so you can come up with the right ideas together.

Don't be afraid to lean on others and invite them into problem-solving conversations. Never solve problems alone. Always bring your inner circle close to the issues so you can rely on their input and perspective.

Make sure you are surrounded by the right people, who think big and think for solutions.

14

Be
A
Sleeper

The average person sleeps about eight hours a night. That's 56 hours of your 168-hour week. If you do the math that's 1/3 of your life that will be spent snoozing. Sleeping is a major part of your life, whether you like it or not. If we spend nearly 1/3 of our life sleeping it is vital that we get it right. In fact, getting 1/3 of this area in our life working well can make the other 2/3rds work even better.

The problem is no one teaches us how to sleep well. Unless you went to school to study sleep, no one even thinks about learning how to sleep better. But this is one skill that quite possibly could affect your life more than anything else. When you learn how to sleep well, you'll set yourself up for a better life in the long run.

All sleep is not created equal. In the case of a good night's rest, quality trumps quantity every time.

Here are a few examples of some sleep patterns from people you've probably heard of...

- Basketball Player, Lebron James sleeps 12 hours a night.
- British Prime Minister, Winston Churchill slept 7 hours a night.
- CEO of PepsiCo., Indra Nooyi sleeps 5 hours a night.
- Founding Father, Benjamin Franklin slept 6 hours a night.
- Amazon Founder, Jeff Bezos sleeps 8 hours a night.
- Golf Player, Tiger Woods sleeps 4-5 hours a night.
- Singer, Mariah Carrey sleeps 15 hours a night when she prepares to sing.

When we retire for the night our bodies actually travel through a sleep journey. Little did you know that you are on a sleep adventure or nightmare depending on where you travel to. And the payoff at our ultimate destination is glorious if you get there. During sleep, your body travels through a complex set of stages. The secret is to make it from N1 to N2 to the ultimate destination of N3. N3 or deep delta-wave sleep is the stage where you get the most rest on your journey. It is a regenerative period where your body heals and repairs itself. If you don't allow your body to get there, your health and productivity begin to suffer. Highly productive people are not sleep-deprived workaholics, in fact, they are quite the opposite. Highly productive people get great sleep thus allowing them to live out their potential.

All sleep is not created equal. In the case of a good night's rest, quality trumps quantity every time. The quality of your sleep will determine the quality of your day. Your preparation to be productive for tomorrow actually starts tonight. Pull back to get good sleep and it will prepare you to go further than you could have gone otherwise. Here are some quick tips to help you be a better sleeper and amp up the quality of your snoozing.

> **"The quality of your sleep will determine the quality of your day."**

Here are 8 great sleeping tips to think about…

LIGHTS OUT

Darkness creates a happier life, at least when it comes to sleep. The darker it is the better off you are. Light has a profound negative effect on our sleep. High exposure to light stimulates our body to stay awake. Our body is tricked into thinking it's time to work, not sleep. Melatonin, a sleep hormone that triggers the brain for sleep, is needed to shut our body down. This hormone causes our muscles to relax, a drop in our body temperature, and feelings of drowsiness. Light inhibits our production of Melatonin which makes it much harder for us to fall asleep. So, bright night lights and lamps are out of the question. Your room needs to be more of a cave and less of a nightclub.

COLDER IS BETTER

The big question is how cold should it be? This has caused more marital problems than any other question in history. It is responsible for angry sleepless nights all around the globe. So, let's solve the debate according to science. Research has concluded that the ideal sleep temperature should be between 60-67 degrees Fahrenheit for adults. There it is, colder temperatures create a hibernation effect on our bodies.

BE CONSISTENT

Your body craves consistency, especially when it comes to sleep. In fact, the more inconsistent you are, the less recovery you'll experience. Our bodies are designed to move in rhythm and when we get out of sync it can cause dissonance with our well-being. It is important that you have a dedicated bedtime that is routinely followed. Studies have shown us that having an expected sleep pattern helps our bodies prepare for great rest.

DRESS UP

What you wear to bed matters. Believe it or not, pajamas can help you sleep better. If you are going to get the most out of your sleep you need to dress for success. Forget the ratty tatty clothes that are barely held together anymore (unless you really love them and they are super comfortable). Dress up for bed. Find some pajamas that trigger your mind that it's time for great sleep. Get some pajamas that make you feel good. Great pajamas set you up for quality sleep

WIND DOWN

You need a wind down to your day, especially in our chaotic culture. Don't run yourself rugged right up until bedtime. Your body needs to transition into a calming effect. It's important for you to have a cool down to your day, just like you need a cool down from a heavy workout. An evening routine before bedtime can help you start the process of quality sleep. The last thing you want to do is watch a thrilling movie before bed, read negative news, eat a huge meal, check email, etc... Don't ramp up your night with stimulating activities while you should be winding down.

CREATE PARADISE

If there is ever anything you should invest in, it's your bedroom. This is probably one of the most crucial rooms in your house. Your bedroom is your sanctuary from the world. It is of the utmost importance that you turn it into your very own paradise. Whatever you need to do to make this place of refuge work for you...do it! Get your favorite mattress, buy sheets and pillows you love, and decorate in a way that creates your ideal ambiance.

THINK SLEEP

The best technique you can use to control your thoughts for sleep is to actually think about sleeping. Visualizing a relaxing scene does wonders for your well-being. Picture yourself resting in your favorite paradise destination. The more you can paint the picture in your mind, the more you will begin to realize the benefits of the actual feeling. Your mind is powerful, it can create the same feelings as if you were actually there. This is your time to mentally go wherever you want to go and recreate your perfect scenario, and it's fun!

FIND YOUR NUMBER

Every person is different when it comes to how much sleep they need. Of course, the generally recommended number is 8 hours. But not everyone is bound to that recommendation. Some require more, some require less. Most people are out of balance when it comes to their perfect number. They either sleep too little or possibly sleep too much. You need to find your ideal number that gives you your best return. Too little sleep can cause drowsiness and mental fogginess, and too much sleep and cause lethargy and apathy. You have to fine-tune what your body requires to function optimally.

15

Leverage
Your
Lungs

I love to play Scrabble. Of course, the point of the game is to use your words very strategically to get the most amount of points based on the value of your letter tiles. The way you use your words determines how high you score, which in turn, determines if you win or lose. Life works much like Scrabble; how we use our words will determine our outcome.

The way we communicate has the power to either:

- Construct or Destruct
- Build or Bulldoze
- Empower or Implode
- Motivate or Mutilate
- Exonerate or Assassinate

Excellent communication makes the difference between average leaders and great leaders. When communication goes down, confusion comes up. If I could spend one day with you and your team, I would be able to tell how successful you will be based on what is communicated. You see, every organization has a language; a dialect in which they communicate. The narrative that is used will determine the result in which it produces.

Words always produce results: good, bad, or indifferent. Words are constantly at work affecting outcomes. Once something is communicated, it is out there. The wave of impact that word has will continue to carry momentum long after it is heard. This is why we play back words and conversations in our heads long after the conversation has been finished. Author Napoleon Hill said, "Think twice before you speak, because your words and influence will plant the seed of either success or failure in the mind of another." Words are truly like seeds that will eventually produce sweet fruits or bitter roots. As leaders, we must be very careful and very intentional about the words we communicate.

Proverbs 18:21 says, "The tongue has the power of death and life." The more respect a person has, the more powerful their words become. What you say, and how you say it, determines what you get and how you get it. You will never see a highly successful leader or organization that communicates from a negative narrative. In fact, the reason they became successful is largely due to communicating life-giving words. However, you will always see struggling leaders and organizations consistently speaking from a negative, life-draining narrative.

Being an effective communicator can make or break your leadership potential. In fact, communication is vital to build your influence and impact. American financier and statesman

Bernard Baruch said, "The ability to express an idea is well nigh as important as the idea itself."

Let me break down my communication formula for you:

Bad Communication + Bad Competency = No Influence
Good Communication + Bad Competency = Terminal Influence
Bad Communication + Good Competency = Limited Influence
Good Communication + Good Competency = Massive Influence

I see a lot of leaders who are good at what they do, but they are not good at communicating what they do. Therefore, their influence is limited. They are not able to show their value because their communication is lacking. As I have coached hundreds of leaders, here are some of the top reasons why people don't communicate well.

TOO HUMBLE

Some people are simply too humble, meaning they think communicating too much is some form of pride. They don't want to appear too pushy or too dominating. But in doing so, they leave opportunity on the table by being too quiet. Humility is a great thing, but being humble doesn't mean you have to be silent. If this is what you struggle with challenge yourself to become more confident and bold in what you have to say...trust yourself. Believe in yourself and the value you bring.

TOO FEARFUL

Many people are silent because they don't want to say something wrong. They fear to mess up their words and say something that will make them look bad. But this fear suppresses their potential to be a better communicator. The only way to get better at communicating is to simply do it a lot. Never allow fear of looking bad or saying something wrong limit your ability to grow your influence. Even though you think you're saving your influence by being silent it is only sabotaging your influence in the long run. Conquer your fear and step out! Challenge yourself to have a practice mindset.

TOO FAST

Speaking without thinking plagues many leaders. We all know people who think while they speak. They process as they proclaim. Though there is good in communicating to bring clarity to your own thoughts be careful not to speak too fast without thinking through it first. You can quickly lose credibility by always having something to say without it being worth saying. Don't speak just to speak, speak because you have something meaningful to add

> **"Be slow to speak and quick to listen so you know how to respond."**

to the conversation. Be slow to speak and quick to listen so you know how to respond. Slow down and if you have something to say write it down on your notepad before you blabber it out without substance.

Challenge yourself to listen. A leader that never listens will never be listened to.

TOO SLOW

On the flip side of being too fast to speak some can be too slow to speak. They take way too long to formulate thoughts and put them into words. If this is your challenge you have to develop speed thinking skills. Challenge yourself to think faster. To do this, make sure you are rested up, prepared, and enter meetings with focus and energy. I coach many leaders to have a pre-meeting pep rally for themselves. Go into a secluded area and give yourself a pep-talk and spark your thinking engine. Some like to have a certain ritual like listening to a song that pumps them up, reading a motivational quote that focuses them, a few minutes of silence before starting, etc... Whatever works for you...do it!

Too Unskilled

This too can be a limiting belief people have that keeps them from speaking up. But truly, some people just don't know how to communicate effectively. They feel they have tried and it all comes out wrong. I would encourage those who struggle with this to apply themselves and learn how to be a better communicator. There is no reason you can't develop your skills and get better. Great communicators aren't just born, they are forged through training and experience. You too, can learn, but you're going to have to find resources, coaches, and opportunities for yourself to get better.

With hard work and dedication to learning you can become an awesome communicator. When you start to step out and work on it you will increase your influence over time...I promise, take my word for it!

16

Laugh
Out
Loud

You'll never live life to the fullest if you can't laugh. In fact, laughter is as much of a leadership thing as any other element. Holocaust survivor and founder of Logotherapy Viktor Frankel said, "Humor, more than anything else in the human make-up, can afford an aloofness and an ability to rise above any situation, if only for a few seconds." Even in the midst of the most horrific circumstances, Frankel understood the power that laughter has on our wellbeing.

Laughter is literally like a natural medicine that heals our souls. When we smile and laugh the brain releases dopamine, a powerful neurotransmitter that produces feelings of happiness. It also has been proven to boost immune systems as well as lower blood pressure and increase oxygen intake. We are hard-wired with an internal happiness mechanism that is triggered by a joyful attitude. Numerous studies have discovered that happy people live much healthier and more productive lives.

We must be intentional about laughter and make it part of our everyday experience. Too many people are so serious they have lost the ability to enjoy life. They are so intensely focused that it is slowing down their ability to succeed. It sounds counter-intuitive to think someone can actually become so engrossed that it backfires on them, but it happens all the time with young leaders. Instead of allowing things to happen organically, they are forcing change which causes disharmony with others and their circumstances. You have to be willing to move in rhythm with your environment in order to succeed. Enjoyment is key to longevity. You may be great at the short game, but if you can't play the long game you'll eventually lose.

Here are some tips to keep yourself full of joy as you play the long game of success.

LAUGH AT YOUR BUSYNESS

Too often we go without laughter when life is busy and stress-ful. Before long, we realized we haven't LOL'd. This not only has physical repercussions but spiritual ones as well. We have to make sure we make opportunities for laughter in our lives. All work plus no play equals psychological disarray. Take time to get away and laugh. Take time to do things that will refill your energy tank. It's much harder to serve and pour out ourselves if we are crushed by life's challenges. The longer we go without taking a laugh break the more burned out we get. I like how Will Rogers said, "If you find yourself in a hole, the first thing to do is stop digging." Literally getting away just to laugh and enjoy life can do wonders to your well-being. I have heard it said that some people don't just worry occasionally, they worry recreationally. If we can learn to live simpler, we can learn to live happier. It's when we make things harder than they need to be that life becomes harder than it was meant to be. Don't be so busy that you forget to laugh.

LAUGH AT YOURSELF

You are going to mess up. That's right, you are going to do some not-so-smart things in life. If you take yourself too seriously at all times, you are going to become a bitter person. You have to learn to laugh at your mistakes and faults. I'm not making light of our mistakes, just that we need to understand we can't change the past and there's no need to be destroyed because of it. If you can't find humor in your shortcomings, you won't find humor in other people's shortcomings. And that makes for a very miserable life, because you will let yourself down, and others will let you down. Those who can gracefully recover from mistakes will proceed into success. If you are always trying to avoid failures and mistakes you are going to play it too safe. Part of stepping out in faith is having the courage to fail. When we beat ourselves up over our mistakes, we open the door to discouragement. And discouragement literally "disses" our courage to move forward. William Arthur Ward said, "To make mistakes is human; to stumble is commonplace; to be able to laugh at yourself is maturity."

LAUGH AT YOUR CIRCUMSTANCES

Staying grateful and appreciative is one of the greatest ways to keep yourself in line. When we let our attitude be one of thanksgiving, we tend to be much happier. It is when we feel we deserve something that we are in danger of being ungrateful. Ungratefulness turns into selfishness, and selfishness turns into pride. Pride keeps us from our fullest potential. Having an attitude of gratitude ensures we are on the road to success. Circumstances will constantly be changing over time. If we don't keep ourselves humble in the midst of the changing times we will be subject to the storms of life. We can't control what we go through, but we can control how we go through it. The difference between successful people and unsuccessful people is their response to circumstances. American Novelist Raymond Chandler said, "Ability is what you're capable of doing. Motivation determines what you do. Attitude determines how well you do it."

> **"We can't control what we go through, but we can control how we go through it."**

Helen Keller said, "Keep your face to the sunshine and you cannot see a shadow." Every day, your mind is a battlefield where a war takes place. If we give up and surrender to the fight, we become a victim to our worst thoughts. We must remain steadfast in our thinking and be on guard at all times. If we continue to think healthy positive thoughts despite our feelings, the day will come when we will feel like it. We have to develop healthy positive habits day by day. Do not be led by your feelings, but lead your feelings. Keep a joyful laughter in the midst of your challenges and you'll become stronger from it.

17

Play
More

As children, we are born with a dreamer mindset. A drive to play, to ask questions, to create, and to enjoy life. Kids treat the world as their playground. My wife Erin, and I have four kiddos who amaze me at their ability to turn an empty room into an amusement park in their mind. They can turn the bathtub into an ocean. They can turn the bed into a spaceship that takes them on a joy ride across the galaxy.

Kids are innovative dreamers who aren't limited by their physical environment. It reminds me of a story I heard about Walt Disney as a kid. One day he drew faces on his flowers during an art class. When the teacher instructed him that flowers do not have faces he responded, "Mine do." Walt Disney was a dreamer who never stopped dreaming even as an adult. As a result of His dreams, Disney has become one of the largest and most successful companies on the planet. Our family just recently went to a trip to Disney World in Florida and I was amazed at the experience. During a play in the Magic Kingdom, Mickey Mouse had the crowd chant, "Dreams come true." Our youngest daughter Allie, screamed at the top of her lungs,

"Dweams com twue" and at that exact moment, fireworks shot out of Cinderella's Castle. Her eyes were as wide as hubcaps when it happened. The rest of the night she went on and on about her ability to cause fireworks to shoot out into the air all because she really did believe.

Somehow we have lost the magic of being a kid as we get older. The playground turns into a prison. Before we know it we don't play anymore–we work. And we work as a slave to a system that produces burnout. The excitement that once couldn't keep us in the bed now becomes a mundane discipline just to get out of it. Instead of anticipating the day with wonder and amazement, we wander through the day with more to do than we have time for. Life becomes about tasks and less about toys. Children get it, adults don't. The older we get the less we play. And the less we play the more we pay for it.

Play is what makes life enjoyable. It's what balances our well-being. All work and no play equal psychological disarray. If you did a study on some of the most success-

> **"All work and no play equal psychological disarray."**

ful people, you would find several common denominators among them. One of the denominators is that they all have hobbies they are passionate about. For example:

• Former President, George W. Bush, is an avid painter
• Actress Susan Sarandon calls herself a ping-pong propagandist
• Billionaire Richard Branson's favorite sport is kiteboarding
• Investor Warren Buffet plays a lot of online bridge

- Inventor Albert Einstein loved to sail
- Apple Founder Steve Jobs played guitar
- Actress Angelina Jolie collects daggers
- Google Co-Founder Sergey Brin does trapeze

Hobbies allow us to escape from work and replenish our quality of life. When we engage in an enjoyable hobby, we are investing in our well-being. Having healthy creative outlets allows us to decompress from stress. Everyone should have a hobby that they can get lost in at times. The oscillation from work to play generates more creative energy. Remember playing cars as a kid with Hot Wheels, micro-machines, or whatever type of toy you had? You could set up tracks with three-hundred-sixty-degree loops right in the middle.

These loops would create momentum for the car to keep going until it reached the finish line. As soon as the car made its way down the loop, it would pick up an extreme amount of force to keep moving. In the same way, hobbies create a propelling loop that gives us the mental and physical strength to keep persevering. They reward us with improved creativity, emotional restoration, self-confidence, stress relief, social connection, idea generation, leadership lessons, and broader awareness. Simply put, hobbies are extremely good for the soul and the mind.

There is a powerful correlation between our work and our play. The less we play the worse our work, and the more we play, the better our work. Most people live that last statement out in reverse. They think the more they play the worse their work and the less they play the better their work.

Dr. Bowen White, physician and founding member of the National Institute for Play, a nonprofit that supports research into the power of play said, "We all come into the world knowing how to play," adding that "As adults, we shouldn't feel like we have to grow out of it." He also stated that in their research they found that play is essential to our health.

So many world-changing ideas and solutions have been conceived during recreation. For instance, 3M inventor Art Fry had his breakthrough moment while on the company's private golf course when he got the idea for post-it notes. George de Mestral was on a hunting trip when he noticed burdock burs sticking to his clothes and his dog's fur. Curiosity led him to study the burs to figure out why they stuck so well. He used what he learned to create Velcro.

Ideas come to us more frequently when we are in a relaxed state of mind. The word recreation means "to create again or renew." Recreation always precedes creation. When you are fresh, you are at your best. Make sure you are investing time in your leisurely pursuits for a well-rounded life experience. Author James A. Michener said, "The master in the art of living makes little distinction between his work and his play, his labor and his leisure, his mind and his body, his information and his recreation, his love and his religion. He hardly knows which is which. He simply pursues his vision of excellence at whatever he does, leaving others to decide whether he is working or playing. To him he's always doing both."

To be an effective leader, embrace work and recovery as equally important responsibilities.

18

Stay On Target

Many obstacles will test a leader's ability to keep their eyes on the prize. We face challenges every day that can easily get our focus off of what really matters. Daniel Boone explored the great wilderness of Tennessee and Kentucky. It was Boone who marked the Wilderness Road that brought settlers into the new land. He often wandered over vast areas of forest, living off the land and dodging arrows. Even though he navigated uncharted territory, he kept on his mission to become familiar with the land. Once, he was asked if he had ever been lost. He replied, "No." He said that he had never been lost, but he did admit that he was "a mite confused once for about three or four days though!"

Leaders have to be the ones who stay on target even when things get shaky. They have to become the anchor in the storm for their team. When everyone else begins to panic and allow negative thinking to consume them, leaders have to be the ones to display genuine optimism. Gilbert Arland said, "When an archer misses the mark, he turns and looks for the fault within himself. Failure to hit the bull's-eye is never the fault of the target. To improve your aim–improve yourself."

You have to keep yourself focused on the target at all times. Keep your eyes on the objectives, not the obstacles. If you expect your team to commit themselves to the vision, then you must demonstrate your own high commitment to the vision. You accomplish this through a focused personal dedication to stay on target and keep your eyes forward to the future, not backward to the past. Thomas J. Watson said, "Nothing so conclusively proves a man's ability to lead others, as what he does from day to day to lead himself."

Here are 3 ways to keep your team on target:

KEEP YOURSELF FOCUSED

When you, as the leader, drift from the mission, others will begin to drift from the mission. Do what you must to keep yourself aligned with passion and dedication. Your first responsibility is to yourself. If you are not in a healthy place it's very difficult to lead others to a healthy place. This is why you have to be intentional about starting and ending your day with life-giving routines. Don't wake up at the last minute possible, turn on negative news, and frantically start your work day. Rather, give yourself time to think, read, or watch something inspirational, and plan your day so you are prepared for the challenges to come. Similarly, end your day with healthy routines that help you unwind, relax, and rejuvenate for the next day.

Every day you bring a version of yourself to work. It's your choice who that person will be. It will either be the best version of yourself, the worst version of yourself, or the caught-in-the-middle version of yourself. Chances are that different situations cause a different version of yourself to appear. But to be truly successful, we need to strive to bring the boldest, most focused, and energized version of ourselves to all that we do. It's when we are truly present that we become a great leader.

KEEP THE TARGET VISIBLE

People need to be reminded of what they are working towards. Vision blurs. Unfortunately, vision blurs over time. We begin to naturally lose enthusiasm. People need to be continually reminded about why they are doing what they are doing. Government official Paul Nitze said, "One of the most dangerous forms of human error is forgetting what one is trying to achieve." A leader has to be the one to keep the vision alive by keeping it visible as often as they can. Did you know that, according to research, one of the top reasons people don't reach their goals is due to lack of visibility? Simply seeing the goal and being reminded of it keeps us hyper-focused on our mission.

You must be able to give them a clear depiction of your target. When a leader paints a sure picture of *why* they are doing what they are doing and *where* they are going, a team can harmonize with one another and with the organization. The clearer the vision, the more productive people will be.

Christopher Wren, one of the greatest architects in London, was commissioned to build Saint Paul's Cathedral after the great fire of 1666. While observing three bricklayers working on a scaffold, Wren asked, "What are you doing?"

The first man who was crouched replied, "Just making a living."

The second man who was halfway standing said, "Just building a wall."

The third man who was working hard and determined said, "Creating a cathedral for the Almighty."

Indeed, the last man knew what his true work was all about; his vision was clear.

KEEP GOING

Endurance is the key to overcoming obstacles. Success is not a short sprint, it is a marathon. Those who hang in there the longest are the ones who taste the sweetness of victory. It will always take longer than you thought and be harder than you anticipated. Without the discipline of patience, you will give up and bail out from your pursuit of success. Our lives are the same way. The journey of a successful life must be built on patience. Thinking you will be an overnight success is not reality. In fact, I once heard it said that anyone can become an overnight success after 20 years of hard work. The journey to success is a daily process of pushing on even when it gets tough.

Patience is the name of the game. But you can't truly have patience unless you couple it with endurance. Endurance is the ability to have patience, and patience is the ability to endure. So to experience a life as an entrepreneur of your own success you must extract endurance within yourself. You have to reach deep within and live from a place of purpose and dedication to your cause. If you don't have an unwavering sense of determination you will give up when things get shaky...and things always get shaky. Radio personality Paul Harvey used to say, "You can tell you're on the road to success; it's uphill all the way." Remember The Tortoise and the Hare: "Slow and steady wins the race."

William Arthur Ward wrote these great words of advice:

Believe while others are doubting
Plan while others are playing
Study while others are sleeping.
Decide while others are delaying
Prepare while others are daydreaming
Begin while others are procrastination
Work while others are wishing
Save while others are wasting
Listen while others are talking
Smile while others are frowning
Commend while others are criticizing
Persist while others are quitting

(19)

Detox From Overworking

Leadership can cause addictive behaviors. These addictions seem harmless but prove to be devastating to our influence and impact, not to mention our well-being. As I coach many leaders spanning different continents, I see these behaviors everywhere. I want to have an intervention and help you overcome these addictive behaviors that may be infiltrating your life without you even knowing.

Let's tackle one of the most addictive behaviors:

Overworking

The Symptoms:
When you keep telling yourself it's just this project; it's just this month, it's just this phase, it's just this season, again and again, you're an overworking addict. You don't know it, and you keep telling yourself you're not, but…you are.

The excuse you tell yourself is, "It's not my choosing. I don't want this!" But you do. If you really didn't want it, you would take drastic steps to change it. I have some hard truth for you… if you really wanted to lose weight…you would. If you really wanted to save more money…you would. If you really wanted to clean the garage…you would. We do the things we really want to do without any excuse that gets in our way. Most likely you are a high achiever, which means, if you really wanted something, you would figure out a way to make it happen…period.

Overworking actually causes you to underperform. Your focus, energy, body, and quality of work can only take so much before it starts to break down. Without moments of rest and recovery, you'll lose yourself and your sharpness as you descend into burnout. You won't know it though…it's like the frog in the kettle of boiling water story. You'll grow accustomed to your low levels and forget what it was like to operate at peak performance. You won't recognize it, admit it, or feel it, but you'll lose your edge over time and it will be noticed by everyone but you.

So, how do we fix this addiction and overcome overworking?

The Detox:
There are 3 leadership pills you need to take to treat your addiction:

1) Prioritizationol
2) Delegationine
3) Boundriesipan

PRIORITIZATIONOL

This is a fast-working treatment that will cause you to prioritize your responsibilities. You can't do it all, let me repeat that for those in the back of the room…YOU CAN'T DO IT ALL! I hope you heard that. I work with many organizations and have worked with many over the last twenty years in leadership coaching and everyone…I repeat…everyone I have worked with typically is trying to do way too much! Did you get that again…they are trying to do too much and it is causing stress, turnover, burnout, and distraction in the team.

Remember, when everything is a priority, nothing is. You have to make the main thing the main thing and keep focused on what matters most. Every little side project, one-off, small task, shiny object, or new shower idea only makes everything move slower in the long run. You have to eliminate all the unnecessary or push it off till a later day when you can prioritize it or it will kill your productivity.

Prioritizing your schedule, projects, meetings, tasks, etc…is insanely hard, this is why most don't do it well. In fact, you have to make time to prioritize your stuff or your stuff will prioritize you. Ben Franklin said, "For every minute spent in organizing, an hour is earned." Organize your stuff painstakingly. And give yourself and your team permission to do less. You have to think progressively not momentarily. Don't let your drive and ambition outrun your energy and well-being. Be patient as you play the long game of success.

DELEGATIONINE

The next pill you need to take in order to detox your leadership is a giant dose of delegation. Most leaders I work with are not good at this…or not as good as they think they are. Most likely I can almost guarantee you are holding on to things you need to delegate right now. You are telling yourself a few excuses for not delegating. Here are the most common:

- "No one can do it as good as me."
- "My team is too overwhelmed as it is. I can't give them more."
- "I won't have anything to do if I give all my stuff away."
- "They are not ready to take on what I need to give them."

Never stop growing your responsibility; instead, increase your delegation ability. The higher you go as a leader, the greater the need to be an amazing delegator. You can't do it all, and great leaders know this. They don't pretend to be superheroes; they learn how to delegate more effectively. Your leadership capacity is a direct result of your delegation strategy. Let me say that again…YOUR LEADERSHIP CAPACITY IS A DIRECT RESULT OF YOUR DELEGATION STRATEGY. You can only go as high as your willingness to let go. As my mentor Dr. John C. Maxwell, always taught me, you have to give up in order to go up. You need to make sure you have a delegation plan, knowing what the next 10% of your workload you will unload.

BOUNDRIESIPAN

Draw lines around your day. Without clear boundaries, your day will never end. And your day must end for you to recover and rejuvenate. If you're always available, you'll never be sustainable. Too many leaders blur their boundary lines, causing them to drift off into an imbalanced life. Give your day hard starts and hard stops to keep from losing yourself. Draw lines around your limits, or you'll limit your energy and focus. If you have no boundaries to your workload, you'll literally get lost in a sea of work. There is only so much a person can do before they start to lose productivity, focus, energy, decision-making ability, fulfillment, etc...

The longer you work without boundaries the worse you actually become. Overworking backfires on you, causing underperformance. You think you are getting more done, but you start moving slower, making mistakes, making poor decisions, and it's causing you more work. You have to manage your energy, not just your time. The only way to be in peak performance is to make sure you are living within the boundaries of what you should handle...did you get that? I didn't write "what you could handle..." You could work 14-hour days and all through the weekend...there is nothing stopping you from doing that...but just because you could, NEVER means you should!

I hope this is helpful to your leadership addiction of overworking. If you suffer from this, which you probably do to some extent...GET INTENTIONAL, GET OUT OF IT...AND GET HELP!

(20)

Get Feedback

Feedback is essential to reach your potential. It provides you with insights into your performance, skills, and areas for improvement. Without honest and meaningful feedback from those around you, it can be nearly impossible to develop as a leader. You cannot truly be your best without a means of receiving helpful feedback.

The problem is that many leaders do not actively seek out feedback. Therefore they are unable to improve to their fullest potential. You cannot improve that which you are unaware of. You can only get better if you truly know what you need to improve.

All feedback we receive must be filtered through a process to ensure its maximum impact on our growth. All feedback is not necessarily the right feedback. We have to understand the variables that play into knowing how to receive feedback properly. I have developed a series of five questions you have to run all communication through as you process it...I call it the Feedback Filter.

Let's break down the five questions:

WHO SAID IT?

You have to filter feedback first from who gave it to you. The source of feedback can have a significant impact on the effectiveness and usefulness of the feedback. Feedback from someone who has the right to speak can be highly valuable as it comes from a position of knowledge and experience. This feedback can provide a better understanding of the strengths and weaknesses and help you make the necessary improvements.

On the other hand, feedback from someone who does not understand the situation may not be as useful or relevant. Such feedback can be biased, uninformed, and may not align with your goals and aspirations for the future.

WHAT WAS SAID?

Always consider the content of the feedback you receive. Evaluate whether it's specific, actionable, and relevant to your role as a leader. Try to find the gold nugget you need to extract from what is being said. Receiving feedback can be a challenging experience, especially if you don't agree with the feedback being provided. However, it's important to remember that feedback is an opportunity for growth and development, even if you don't fully agree with it.

Here are some tips for receiving feedback, even if you don't agree with it:

Listen actively: Give the person providing the feedback your undivided attention. Make eye contact, nod your head, and ask questions to show that you are engaged and interested in what they have to say.

Clarify and ask questions: If you don't fully understand the feedback or disagree with it, ask the person providing the feedback to clarify or provide examples. This can help you gain a better understanding of their perspective and identify areas for improvement.

Avoid becoming defensive: It's natural to feel defensive when receiving feedback, especially if it's critical or negative. However, becoming defensive can prevent you from truly hearing and considering the feedback. Instead, take a deep breath, stay calm, and try to remain open-minded.

Reflect on the feedback: You may not completely agree with all that is said, but you must reflect on what may be contributing to the other person's perception of your behavior. Reflect on the feedback objectively and consider if there may be some truth to it, even if you don't fully agree. Look for patterns or trends in the feedback that may point to areas for improvement.

WHY WAS IT SAID?

It's also important to consider the intention behind the feedback. Feedback that is provided constructively with the intention of helping you improve can be highly beneficial. However, feedback that is provided with the intention of putting you down or making you feel inferior can be harmful and unproductive.

Here are signs of constructive feedback or destructive feedback:

Constructive feedback is balanced and fair, acknowledging both positive and negative aspects of the situation. Destructive feedback is often one-sided and ignores any positive contributions or achievements.

Constructive feedback focuses on specific behaviors or actions that can be improved, while destructive feedback attacks the person and their character.

Constructive feedback is relevant to the situation and objective in nature, while destructive feedback may be based on personal biases or emotions.

Constructive feedback is specific and actionable, with suggestions for improvement. Destructive feedback is vague, unhelpful, and doesn't offer any guidance on how to improve.

HOW MANY TIMES HAS IT BEEN SAID?

Factoring in how many times you have received the same feedback is an important consideration when it comes to improving as a leader. Consistent feedback from multiple sources is a strong indication that there may be an area for improvement that needs to be addressed. When you receive consistent feedback from multiple sources, it can help you identify patterns in your behavior that may be impacting your effectiveness as a leader.

If the feedback you are receiving is new and has never been communicated by anyone else, you need to factor that in as well. It certainly does not discredit the feedback, it is just an indicator of how important or urgent your response to the feedback should be. Pay attention to how often you receive similar feedback.

Now, What Are You Going To Do?

It is not enough to simply receive feedback; you must also take action on it to make meaningful changes and improve as a leader. Knowledge without action is useless. The only way you can improve is to take action and apply new behaviors.

Here are some tips on what to do with the feedback you receive:

Embrace the feedback and acknowledge that there is room for improvement. Recognize that the feedback is a gift that can help you become a better leader.

Identify specific behaviors to change based on the feedback you have received. Be specific and actionable in your approach.

Develop a plan of action for changing these behaviors. Set realistic and achievable goals, and establish a timeline for achieving them.
Seek support from mentors, colleagues, or coaches who can provide guidance and accountability. Share your plan of action with them, and ask for feedback and support as you work to change your behaviors.

Monitor your progress regularly to see how you are doing. Celebrate successes, and make adjustments as needed.

Changing yourself based on feedback takes time, and it may not happen overnight. Be patient with yourself, and continue to work toward your goals. Utilize the Feedback Filter, and you'll know no limits to your leadership growth.

Conclusion

Thanks for journeying through Leadership Starts With You. I hope it has helped you somehow, someway, go to a new level in your leadership ability. I have found that when you invest in your leadership ability, you're directly investing in the future you desire to experience.

Great leaders are always advancing their leadership ability to the next level. They never stop challenging themselves to reach new heights. They know the secret to success is the capacity to lead well. In fact, true success is simply an overflow of great leadership. Yet, so many leaders and organizations feel frustratingly stuck. They are striving for success but aren't gaining any traction into growth. Their solution...work harder. But in doing so, they are just spinning their wheels in the mud.

This is where I come in. I help individuals and companies break through their limiting factors and elevate their success. A Hay Group study of Fortune 500 companies found that 21%–40% utilize Executive Coaching; Coaching was used as standard leadership development for elite executives and talented up-and-comers. An internal report of the Personnel Management Association showed that when training is combined with coaching, individuals increase their productivity by an average of 86% compared to 22% with training alone.

I have been working with leaders for over eighteen years. I have been personally mentored by the #1 leadership expert in the world, Dr. John C. Maxwell, as a certified coach, speaker, and trainer on the John Maxwell Team. I have worked with Fortune 500 companies, entrepreneurs, non-profits, and individuals who have leveled up their success through my coaching.

I would love the opportunity to help you and/or your team develop their leadership capacity. Please check out my website with great leadership tips updated weekly and get a free copy of my book 50 Powerful Quotes To Take You Somewhere Better.

If you would like to level up through coaching/training here is the process to get started:

CONTACT ME

Set up a time so we can connect and discover what the next level is for you, your team, and your organization. We will engage with your specific leadership challenges and needs, in order to move upward together. Email: John@johnbarrettleadership.com

CUSTOMIZE YOUR EXPERIENCE

My leadership coaching is designed to take you from exactly where you are to the next level. You will not find prepackaged and predetermined routines, but rather a leadership plan customized to fit your unique situations.

COACH YOUR LEADERSHIP

Once we have discovered your challenges and customized your plan, we will start to empower your leadership performance.

This is where the magic happens as we deliver leadership coaching that will get you to the next level.

CLIMB TO NEW LEVELS

When leaders go to a whole new level, their success goes to a whole new level. Investing in your leadership development will increase your impact, influence, ideas, and income. Being coached allows you to soar to new heights.

ABOUT THE AUTHOR

John is a sought after leadership coach, speaker, and trainer. He has been living and teaching leadership for over twenty years. John has been personally mentored by world renown leadership expert, Dr. John C. Maxwell, and a host of other highly successful leaders. He has coached Fortune 500 companies, entrepreneurs, non-profits, and individuals who desire to level up their success.

John has been interviewed on radio programs, podcasts, blogs, and many other platforms, reaching over 200,000 listeners. He is dedicated to guiding others to the next level on their leadership journey.

5 Ways To Get A Raise

LEADERSHIP
WORKSHOPS
Develop The Tools You Need To Lead

SCHEDULE NOW ›

 CONFLICT RESOLUTION
Create A Conflict Compass To Help Navigate Challenges.

 COMMUNICATION
Develop An Organizational Narrative For Your Team.

 INNOVATION
Discover The Strategies To Help Foster Growth.

 ACCOUNTABILITY
Discover The Guardrails Of Accountability.

 TEAMWORK
Work Together With Shared Core Values.

 PROBLEM SOLVING
Create A Culture Of Breakthrough Thinkers.

 john@johnbarrettleadership.com   765-318-6677   www.JohnBarrettLeadership.com

Get The Latest Episode Today

www.CoffeeWithLeaders.com

Made in United States
Troutdale, OR
02/17/2024

17770817R00099